CW00863809

FOOD Fit For a FAMILY

the Kuznia Family CookBook

Dear Kids,

I wanted to put this cookbook together for you kids so that you can have all of the recipes you grew up with available to you when you're on your own. I hope this cookbook helps you remember the times we shared together over the dinner table. The traditions we had. The memories we shared over food.

In this cookbook, you will find all of our favorite recipes. The recipes that we make time and time again. I collected these recipes over the years, but I have altered almost every single one to make them either easier, bigger, less expensive, or healthier. You know, to make them *Food Fit for a Family*.

During the course of my life, I have read a bunch of information on health and nutrition. With so many contradictory viewpoints out there, it's hard to make heads or tails out of anything. So, do what works for you. These recipes can be made as healthy as you want them. For instance, I use raw milk cheese instead of regular cheese, grassfed organic beef instead of conventional beef, organic vegetables instead of regular produce, etc. You get the idea. I don't label the ingredients as such in the recipes because I find that to be pretentious.

What I've found, more than anything, is that any food homemade, with love, is the best kind of health food out there. Happiness is healthy.

All of you kids have always been open to eating pretty much anything. With the exception of very few things featured in this cookbook (why won't you eat the Beef and Bulgur Salad, Ezra? Why?), you kids eat pretty much all of it. Our table is filled with a family that enjoys food and really loves to eat.

This is our cookbook, dear children. From me to you.

Enjoy.

Love,
mom

Contents

Italian Chicken Soup

Creamy Cabbage and Bacon Soup

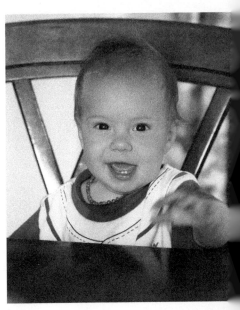

soups

I love making this recipes on cold winter days when we don't have anywhere to go. I make it in the late morning and it cooks slowly in the oven all day and is ready in time for supper. The flavors blend together so nicely and give the stew a rich, hearty taste.

BEEF STEW

1 lb stew meat, cut into chunks
1 onion, chopped into large pieces
6 cloves garlic, chopped
14.5 oz can diced tomatoes
2 tsp dried thyme
Salt and pepper to taste
2 bay leaves
6 cups of beef or chicken stock
1 cup diced carrots
1 cup diced celery
2 cup diced potatoes

Preheat oven to 250 degrees.

In Dutch oven, cook stew meat and onion for about 5 minutes. Add garlic. Add tomatoes, seasonings, and stock.

Cover and cook in the oven for at least 4 hours.

Remove pot from oven. Place on stove over medium low heat.

Add vegetables. Cover and cook for another hour.

This recipe came to us by way of my friend Sally. It was a recipe from the Pioneer Woman blog that Sally shared on Facebook. I dumbed the recipe down a bit (as I always do), so it is easier to make. We are all in love with this soup. (The ditalini pasta is kind of hard to find, but I like to use it anyway, since it's different. You can use any kind of noodle though.)

ITALIAN CHICKEN SOUP

16 oz ditalini pasta
Shredded chicken (see page 18)
8 cups chicken broth
1 onion, diced
2 green bell peppers, diced
2 stalks celery, diced
2 jalapenos, diced
28 oz can whole tomatoes
2 cups heavy cream
1 T oregano
Salt and pepper to taste

Cook pasta according to package directions, being sure not to overcook. Drain and rinse in cold water to cool.

Dice the canned whole tomatoes and return to their juice. Set aside.

In a large saucepan, saute onion, green pepper, celery, and jalapenos for about 10 minutes. Add chicken broth, shredded chicken, and tomatoes with their juice.

Bring to a boil, then reduce to a simmer. Add cooked pasta, cream, oregano. Salt and pepper to taste.

I've been making this recipe every year for Christmas since your dad and I were newly married. It's one of our many Kuznia family traditions. This soup is warm and creamy and will always remind me of Christmas.

CHRISTMAS CORN CHOWDER

1 onion, chopped
1 red bell pepper, diced
1 potato, diced
8 oz bacon, cut up
2 cups chicken broth
1 cup milk
1 can creamed corn
1 cup frozen corn
Shredded chicken (see page 18)
1 tortilla, cut into 1" squares
Salt and pepper to taste

In a large saucepan, saute onion, bell pepper, potato, and bacon for 5 minutes. Stir in remaining ingredients (except for tortilla). Cook for 30 minutes. Add tortilla and cook for 5 minutes more.

Salt and pepper to taste.

After sampling this soup at Fresh and Natural Foods, instead of buying it (because it's crazy expensive to buy homemade soups at a health food store), I wrote down all the ingredients that were used and created my own version at home. Yum!

RED THAI CHICKEN CURRY SOUP

1 onion, diced
1 sweet potato, cubed
Shredded chicken (see page 18)
1 T cilantro
4 cups chicken broth
1 can coconut milk
1 T red curry paste
1 T cornstarch
Salt and pepper to taste

In a large saucepan, saute onion. Add everything else and bring to a boil. Then, simmer for about 30 minutes and serve!

This is a good, hearty recipe that serves as a full meal for us. We make it a lot in the winter. In any of these recipes, whenever I say "salt to taste", I mean "SALT TO TASTE!" Since we use homemade, unsalted chicken broth, you're going to have to bring out some of that flavor by adding at least two teaspoons of salt. (Adjust accordingly if using packaged chicken broth.)

SOUTHWESTERN CHICKEN BARLEY CHILI

14.5 oz can diced tomatoes
15 oz can tomato sauce
2 cups chicken broth
1 cup barley
4 cups water
1 T chili powder
2 tsp cumin
1 tsp oregano
Shredded chicken (see page 18)
15 oz can black beans
2 cups frozen corn
Salt to taste

In a large saucepan, combine all the ingredients except the black beans and corn. Bring to a boil and simmer for 40 minutes.

Add the black beans and corn. Simmer for 5 more minutes.

Salt to taste (this means use a good amount of salt, please).

The chili will thicken considerably upon cooling, so add more water if reheating.

I don't remember where this recipe came from, but I like to make it because it's a really good way to use cabbage. We were surprised at how good it was when we first had it. (Just a note: I always use turkey bacon whenever bacon is called for.)

CREAMY CABBAGE AND BACON SOUP

8 oz bacon, cut up
1 onion, diced
2 carrots, diced
2 stalks celery, diced
2 cloves garlic, chopped
15 oz can cannellini beans, drained
4 cups chicken broth
1/2 small head cabbage, chopped
1 tsp oregano
1 bay leaf
1/4 cup milk
Salt and pepper to taste

In a large saucepan, cook bacon. Add the onion, carrots, and celery and saute until tender, about 10 minutes. Add garlic.

Puree half of the beans with some of the chicken stock.

Add the rest of the chicken stock, beans, pureed beans, cabbage, oregano, and bay leaf. Bring to a boil, then reduce to a simmer until the cabbage is tender, about 10 minutes.

Season with salt and pepper.

Oh, how I remember eating this soup when I was pregnant with Solomon. No other food tasted so good! All I wanted was some good tomato soup, and this definitely hit the spot. I like to eat it when not pregnant as well. It is just an all around great soup for any occasion!

CREAMY CURRY TOMATO LENTIL SOUP

1 cup red lentils
2-1/2 cups water
2 tsp ginger powder
2 tsp cinnamon
1 tsp curry powder
1 quart tomato soup
1 can coconut milk
Salt to taste

Place the lentils, water, ginger, cinnamon, curry powder, and tomato soup into a large saucepan and bring to a boil. Lower the heat to a simmer, partly cover, and cook until the lentils are very soft (about 20 minutes).

Add coconut milk and salt to taste.

This soup always reminds me of when Ocean made it for our short lived 2012 YouTube video series on you Kuznia kids cooking. Ezra made lasagna. Peace made pizza. And Ocean made this soup. All of you kids have been very good in the kitchen, even at a young age.

POTATO LEEK SOUP

4 leeks, sliced
3 potatoes, cubed
4 cups chicken broth
1 cup cream
1 cup milk
Salt and pepper to taste

In a large saucepan, saute leeks for 20 minutes. Add the potatoes and broth. Bring to a boil, then simmer for 45 minutes. Puree.

Add the cream and milk and heat through. Salt and pepper to taste.

I asked Sarah R. for this recipe after tasting it at some gathering she hosted. She is one of the best cooks that I know. And this soup is so amazing, I can't even begin to describe how good it is. It is beyond compare. We make it once a week throughout autumn with the butternut squash that we harvest from our garden.

WORLD'S BEST SQUASH SOUP

4 cups butternut squash, cubed
3 cups chicken broth
1 cup apple cider (or apple juice)
1 apple, peeled and diced
1 cup carrots, chopped
1 onion, diced
1/4 tsp allspice
1/4 tsp nutmeg
1/4 tsp cloves
1/2 tsp crushed red pepper
Salt and pepper to taste

1/4 cup maple syrup
1/2 cup butter
1 cup cream

Place all ingredients (except syrup, butter, and cream) in a large saucepan. Bring to a boil, cover, and simmer until tender, around 20-30 minutes.

Add the syrup, butter, and cream.

Puree soup and serve.

This is a boring recipe, but I'm including it in here because it is something you need to know. This is how we get the shredded chicken that we use in our chicken recipes. I do it this way because it is more cost effective. (If you don't want to do this, you can also use 2 boneless skinless chicken breasts, cut up, in it's place.) This is also how we get our broth. It's important to remember that this is an unsalted broth. You will usually need to add decent amount of salt to make a nice salty broth.

HOW TO BOIL A CHICKEN

1 whole chicken
4 quarts water
2 T vinegar

Put chicken in a super large stockpot with 4 quarts of water and a splash of vinegar.

Bring to a boil, skim off the foam, partly cover and simmer 4-5 hours.

Drain chicken from the stock. (I do this by keeping the lid ajar and draining the stock into another big pot.)

Put the pot of stock in the fridge. Cool overnight. In the morning, skim off the fat and pour into glass jars and freeze. (I've learned to only add 2 cups of broth into a quart jar because if you add too much it will expand and break.)

With the chicken, remove skin and separate from the bones. Divide into 3 or 4 sections, wrap in tinfoil, and freeze until ready to use.

That's it! This is not glamorous work, but it has to be done.

Broccoli with Pasta and Cheese

One Pot Taco Pasta

Artichoke Florentine Pasta

Basil and Chive Lasagna

Pumpkin Lasagna

Baked Chili

Spaghetti Pie

One Pot Taco Pasta

Enchilada Pasta Casserole

Stroganoff

Pastitsio

Orzo Chicken Asiago

Baked Penne with Chicken and Tomatoes

Coconut Curry Chicken Pasta

Pasta with Broccoli and Potatoes

Bacon and Pumpkin Pasta

Caramelized Onion and Garlic Pasta

Penne Pasta with Peas and Mascarpone

Artichoke Florentine Pasta

Green Macaroni and Cheese

Macaroni and Cheese

Lisa T. made us this lasagna after Solomon was born. We all fell instantly in love with it and have been making it regularly ever since. We never seem to make it quite as good as when Lisa made it, but, then again, food never tastes as good as after having a baby or when it is brought to you with love from someone else.

BASIL AND CHIVE LASAGNA

1 lb ground beef
6 cloves garlic, chopped
1 tsp salt
28 oz can crushed tomatoes
1/4 cup fresh basil, chopped
3 T chives, chopped
1/4 cup water
1 cup chicken broth
8 oz cream cheese
8 oz cheddar cheese, shredded
12 lasagna noodles, uncooked

In a large skillet, cook the ground beef, salt, and garlic over medium heat.

Stir in the crushed tomatoes, basil, 2 T chives, and water. Set aside.

In a small saucepan, heat the chicken broth. Add the cream cheese and whisk to blend.

In a 9x13 pan, spread half of the meat mixture. Sprinkle 1/3 of the cheddar cheese over the meat. Lay half of the uncooked noodles over the cheese. Pour cream cheese mixture over noodles. Sprinkle another 1/3 of the cheddar cheese over the cream cheese mixure. Lay the remaining uncooked noodles over the cheese.

Spoon the remaining meat sauce over the noodles. Sprinkle with remaining cheddar cheese. Sprinkle the remaining 1 T chives over the cheese.

Bake, covered, at 400 degrees for 40 minutes. Uncover and bake for another 15 minutes.

For the past several years, during the month of October, we make a new pumpkin recipe using a pumpkin grown from our garden every week. We've made all sorts of pumpkin recipes (some of which you'll find in these pages), and this is one of our favorites.

BEEF AND PUMPKIN LASAGNA

3 cloves garlic, chopped
1 onion, diced
1 carrot, diced
1 red bell pepper, diced
1 lb ground beef
24 oz tomato puree
1 tsp sugar
2 cups cooked pumpkin
10 lasagna noodles, uncooked
15 oz ricotta cheese
8 oz cheddar cheese, shredded

4 T butter
3 T flour
2 cups milk
pinch of salt

In skillet, cook onion and garlic. Add the carrots, red bell pepper, and ground beef. Cook for 5 minutes. Stir in the tomato puree and sugar. Salt to taste. Set aside.

Melt the butter in medium saucepan on low heat. Add the flour and whisk. Slowly whisk in milk until smooth and thickened.

Grease 9x13 pan. Spoon about 1-1/2 cups meat sauce around the base of pan. Layer with 5 lasagna noodles, another 1-1/2 cups of meat sauce, half of the pumpkin, half the ricotta, and half the cheddar cheese.

Layer remaining 5 lasagna noodles, the rest of the meat sauce, pumpkin, and ricotta. Spoon milk sauce over the ricotta and top with cheese.

Cover with foil and bake at 400 degrees for 40 minutes. Remove foil and broil for 5 minutes.

My friend, Kate S., posted this recipe in her short-lived blog (because, hey, who doesn't have a short-lived blog?). It came to her from her grandmother, handwritten on a decades old recipe card. The best part about this recipe is that the noodles at the top are kind of crunchy, which is something that reminds me of grandmas.

BAKED CHILI

1 onion, diced
1 green pepper, diced
1 lb ground beef
1 T oregano
1 tsp basil
1 T chili powder
15 oz can tomato sauce
14.5 oz can diced tomatoes
16 oz pasta
Salt to taste

Cheddar cheese, shredded
Chives

Cook pasta to just under al dente.

In a large skillet, saute onion and green pepper until tender. Add ground beef, and cook until brown. Add spices.

Add the remaining ingredients.

Transfer to casserole dish and bake, uncovered, at 350 degrees for 45 minutes.

Top with cheese and chives, if desired.

This is probably the only recipe in this cookbook that I don't really have a memory for. Everything else, I can think of something to say about it. But as for this... nothing. It's Spaghetti Pie. It's good. It would probably be more like a pie if we cooked it in a pie plate, but we'll stick with that name anyway.

SPAGHETTI PIE

16 oz spaghetti
2 eggs
16 oz cottage cheese
1 lb ground beef
1 onion, diced
25 oz spaghetti sauce
8 oz cheddar cheese, shredded

Cook spaghetti. Mix eggs into hot spaghetti. Form into crust in 9x13 pan.

Spread cottage cheese over crust.

In a skillet, brown beef and onion. Add sauce.

Spread beef mixture over cottage cheese.

Top with shredded cheese.

Bake, uncovered, at 350 degrees for 40 minutes.

This is a hearty meal that is easy to make. Since you are cooking the pasta within the meal (instead of separately), be mindful not to overcook them. Overcooked pasta can easily ruin an otherwise good meal.

ONE POT TACO PASTA

1 lb ground beef
1 onion, diced
2 cloves garlic, chopped
1 cup frozen corn
14.5 oz can black beans, drained
4 oz can diced green chilies
14.5 oz can diced tomatoes
12 oz salsa
16 oz pasta
8 oz cheddar cheese, shredded
Salt and pepper to taste

2 T fresh cilantro

In a large saucepan, cook ground beef, onion, and garlic.

Stir in corn, black beans, and green chilies. Stir in tomatoes, salsa, pasta, and 2 cups water. Bring to a boil, cover, reduce heat, and simmer until pasta is cooked through, about 13-16 minutes.

Remove from heat and top with cheese. Cover until cheese has melted, about 2 minutes.

Top with fresh cilantro, if desired.

Whenever I ask the kids what I should put on the menu for the week, Ezra always says this meal. He included it in the cookbook that his class was doing for school, because it is his favorite. The rest of the family likes it as well. Very rich. Very filling. Very good.

ENCHILADA PASTA CASSEROLE

1 lb ground beef
1/2 tsp chili powder
1/4 tsp cumin
1/4 tsp cayenne
8 oz cream cheese
12 oz enchilada sauce
8 oz cheddar cheese, shredded
1 cup frozen corn
4 oz can diced green chilies
16 oz pasta
Salt and pepper to taste

Boil pasta. Drain.

In skillet, brown ground beef. Add chili powder, cumin, and cayenne.

Add cream cheese until melted and combined.

In a large bowl, combine enchilada sauce, half the cheddar cheese, corn kernels, and diced green chilies. Pour mixture over beef and let simmer 2-3 minutes.

Put mixture in a 9x13 casserole dish and stir in the cooked pasta to combine. Top with remaining cheese.

Bake, uncovered, at 350 degrees for 25 minutes.

I'd never had stroganoff before Jen R. brought it to us after Peace was born. I asked her for the recipe, and now I make it often (although a little differently than the recipe she originally gave me). I know stroganoff is usually served over egg noodles, but since Jen gave it to us over spaghetti, I always do the same. It reminds me of her.

STROGANOFF

1 lb ground beef
1 tsp salt
1/2 tsp pepper
1 onion, diced
4 cloves garlic, chopped
10 oz white mushrooms, sliced
8 oz sour cream
1 cup chicken broth
16 oz spaghetti

Boil spaghetti. Drain. Return to pot.

In a large skillet, brown ground beef with salt, pepper, onion, and garlic. Add mushrooms and cook for 5 minutes.

Add chicken broth and sour cream.

Stir into cooked spaghetti and serve.

This is recipe is an easy version of the Greek dish, Pastitsio. It's has an unusual flavor combination (fennel, cinnamon, and nutmeg) that works well together. With any meal where you are baking noodles after if you've already boiled them, make sure they are boiled just short of al dente. (This is probably 3 minutes short of their regular cook time.)

PASTITSIO

16 oz pasta
1 lb ground beef
25 oz spaghetti sauce
2 tsp cinnamon
1/2 tsp ground fennel
4 eggs
8 oz feta cheese
1 tsp nutmeg
1 cup milk
1 T butter
3 T flour

Boil pasta until just short of al dente. Drain.

In a large skillet, cook beef. Add spaghetti sauce, cinnamon, and fennel.

Make the white sauce: In small saucepan, melt butter on medium heat. Whisk in flour. Slowly add the milk until thickened.

In a bowl, lightly beat the eggs.

Stir 1/2 of the white sauce into lightly beaten eggs, then return to the saucepan. Add 1/2 the feta cheese and the nutmeg.

Layer 1/2 pasta, all of the meat mixture, remaining feta cheese, 1/2 pasta, and all of the white sauce.

Bake, uncovered, at 350 degrees for 30 minutes.

See that red Dutch oven in the picture (and featured throughout this cookbook)? I love that thing. It helps me to make this delicious meal, and many others. I got it as a housewarming gift from Emily, Mike, Erin C., and Sally. It is one of my favorite things ever.

ORZO CHICKEN ASIAGO

Shredded chicken (see page 18)
3 cups chicken broth
1/4 cup white wine
1-1/4 cup orzo pasta, uncooked
1/2 tsp salt
1 tsp basil
1/2 tsp oregano
1 tsp rosemary
1/4 tsp black pepper
1 tomato, diced
1/4 cup green onions, chopped
1 cup frozen peas
8 oz Asiago cheese, shredded
Salt and pepper to taste

Place chicken broth and white wine in large Dutch oven. Bring to a boil. Add the orzo pasta. Reduce heat and simmer for 6 minutes, stirring constantly. Add the chicken, salt, and herbs. Cook for 6 minutes more.

Just as the orzo is finishing, add the tomatoes and green onions. Cook 1 minute more.

Remove pasta mixture from heat. Add the peas.

Stir in the cheese.

Season with salt and pepper.

We like this recipe because it's delicious, and it makes a good amount of food. It's rich and creamy and the sun-dried tomatoes give it a yummy flavor. If I can't find provolone, I just use the regular raw milk cheddar cheese from Trader Joe's that I use for everything.

BAKED PENNE WITH CHICKEN AND TOMATOES

6 T butter
16 oz penne pasta
Shredded chicken (see page 18)
1/2 cup plus 2 T flour
4 cloves garlic, chopped
6 cups milk
10 oz white mushrooms, sliced
8.5 oz oil-packed
    sun-dried tomatoes, drained
8 oz provolone, shredded
1 cup grated Parmesan
Salt to taste

Grease two shallow, 2-quart baking dishes with butter.

Cook pasta until 3 minutes short of al dente. Drain and return to pot.

In a large saucepan, melt butter over medium heat. Add garlic and flour. Whisk the mixture as it cooks, gradually adding milk. Bring to a simmer while continuing to whisk. Add the mushrooms and sun-dried tomatoes and cook for a minute. Remove from burner and gradually stir in provolone and 1/2 cup grated Parmesan.

Add chicken and pasta to the pot, and then divide the mixture between the two baking dishes. Sprinkle the tops with the remaining Parmesan. Bake, uncovered, at 400 degrees for 25 minutes.

For some reason, this recipe claimed to be a soup, but every time I made it, all the liquid got absorbed and it turned out like a pasta. So, that is what it for us. And it is delicious, let me tell you! All of us love this recipe so very much.

COCONUT CURRY CHICKEN PASTA

3 T thai red curry paste
2 - 14 oz cans coconut milk
1 cup chicken broth
1 tsp fish sauce
1 red bell pepper, diced
1 cup snow peas
1 cup frozen peas
2 bundles rice vermicelli noodles
Shredded chicken (see page 18)
1/2 cup green onion, diced
Juice of one lime
Salt to taste

In a large saucepan, heat curry paste, coconut milk, chicken broth, and fish sauce.

Add red bell pepper, snow peas, peas, vermicelli noodles, and chicken. Bring to a boil, reduce heat and simmer for about 8-10 minutes, until noodles have softened.

Add lime juice. Salt to taste.

Garnish with green onions, and serve.

I got this recipe from Kristine, although I can't quite remember why I asked her for it. Kristine is an excellent cook. When she lived here, she would host people for the Rice Street Parade and always make a ton of great food. She has a way of nurturing people through the food that she makes and reminds me of my Great Aunt Rita in that way.

PASTA WITH BROCCOLI AND POTATOES

2 potatoes, cut into 1 inch pieces
1 large bunch broccoli, cut up
16 oz pasta
2 leeks, sliced
2 tsp salt
Pepper to taste
1 head of lettuce
8 oz Fontina cheese, shredded
8 oz bacon

Bring large pot of water to boil. Add potatoes and cook for 10 minutes, then add broccoli and pasta and cook for 8-10 more minutes.

Meanwhile, in a skillet, cook the leeks in some butter. Add the salt and pepper, to taste. Cook about 7 minutes.

Another meanwhile: Fry the bacon, and chop it up.

Cut up lettuce and put into a colander. Reserve 1 cup cooking water, then drain the pasta mixture over the lettuce to wilt it. Return to the pot.

Add the leeks and stir in the reserved water. Stir in the cheese and bacon. Season with more salt and pepper.

This was a meal we originally discovered during our month of finding different recipes for pumpkin every October. Peace especially likes this recipe and asks for it often. It provides the perfect blend of pumpkiny pasta creaminess, and it's orange color makes it seem extra cheesey.

BACON AND PUMPKIN PASTA

16 oz pasta
2 cups pumpkin puree
8 oz cream cheese
1 cup milk
3 cloves garlic, chopped
2 tsp salt
8 oz bacon
1 onion, diced
1/2 cup green onions, chopped

Fry bacon and chop it up.

Cook onion in some butter until caramelized, about 15 minutes.

Boil pasta. Drain and return to pan. Add pumpkin, cream cheese, milk, garlic, and salt. Stir until cream cheese is melted and mixture is warmed through.

Add bacon.

Top with green onions.

I found this recipe in a cooking magazine at my mom's place. I ripped it out, took it home, and have been making it ever since. Once again, I've found myself really enjoying a recipe for it's unique flavor combinations. This meal does not disappoint.

CARAMELIZED ONION AND GARLIC PASTA

2 red onions, thinly sliced
1/4 tsp crushed red pepper flakes
1/4 tsp salt
8 cloves garlic, chopped
2 cups grape tomatoes, halved
1/2 cup balsamic vinegar
1/4 olive oil
16 oz spaghetti
8 oz bacon

Cook onions, red pepper flakes, garlic and salt in some butter for 30 minutes, stirring occasionally. Add the grape tomatoes, balsamic vinegar, and olive oil.

During this time, boil the spaghetti and fry the bacon.

Then, drain the noodles and toss with onion mixture. Sprinkle with cut up bacon.

This is another recipe I ripped out of a magazine from my mom's house. It's delightful. It doesn't make a whole bunch, and I should really alter the recipe to have it make more to feed us all, but for now we make due and snack on other things to fill us up.

PENNE WITH PEAS AND MASCARPONE

8 oz bacon, chopped
1 onion, diced
2 cloves garlic, chopped
1/2 cup white wine
1 cup chicken broth
2 cups frozen peas
1 lb penne pasta
8 oz mascarpone
Juice from 1 lemon
Salt and pepper, to taste

Boil pasta and drain.

In a skillet, cook chopped bacon, onion, garlic for 5 minutes.

Add the white wine and cook until the wine evaporates. Add the chicken broth and bring to a bubble. Add the peas. Salt and pepper to taste.

Stir the mascarpone and lemon juice into the mixture until a sauce forms.

Toss with the penne pasta. It will thicken slightly as it cools.

This is another recipe that I tore out of a cooking magazine at my mom's place. I'm not even sure why she gets those magazines. I don't think she ever uses them. She probably had to order a magazine for a magazine drive or something. Anyway, this is another good one. Rich and creamy.

ARTICHOKE FLORENTINE PASTA

16 oz pasta
6 T butter, divided
4 cloves garlic, chopped
12 oz baby spinach
1/4 cup flour
3 cups milk
3/4 cup grated Parmesan
8 oz cream cheese
1/2 cup white wine
1 tsp salt
1/2 tsp pepper
1/4 tsp cayenne
2 - 14 oz cans artichoke hearts,
    drained and coarsely chopped

Boil pasta and drain.

In Dutch oven, melt 2 T butter over medium heat. Add garlic and cook for 30 seconds. Add spinach and cook for 2-3 minutes or until wilted. Remove from pot.

In the same pot, melt remaining butter. Stir in flour. Gradually whisk in milk. Bring to a boil, stirring constantly. Cook and stir 2-3 minutes or until thickened. Add Parmesan cheese, cream cheese, wine and seasonings. Stir until smooth. Stir in artichoke hearts.

Add pasta to sauce, tossing to coat. Stir in spinach mixture.

On St. Patrick's Day, we used to come up with all sorts of green things to eat: salads, broccoli soup, green peppers. Now we just make this every year because, 1) it's good, 2) we kind of ran out of ideas for other green foods. It's our St. Patrick's Day tradition.

GREEN MACARONI AND CHEESE

16 oz penne pasta
2 T butter + 1/2 cup butter, divided
1 onion, diced
1 jalapeno pepper, diced
6 cups fresh spinach
1/2 cup boiling water
1/2 cup flour
2 cups milk
8 oz cheddar cheese, shredded
8 oz fontina cheese, shredded
Salt to taste

Cook pasta until 3 minutes short of al dente. Drain.

In a small pot, melt 2 T butter and add onions and jalapeno. Cook 7-10 minutes.

In blender, add 6 cups spinach and the boiling water. You will probably need to use a spoon to push the spinach down. Blend to a fine, bright green paste.

In big pot, melt 1/2 cup butter. Add the flour. Gradually stir in milk. Simmer until slightly thickened. Add cheese. Stir until melted.

Add the spinach puree. Pour the pasta into the pot of sauce and add the onions and jalapeno mixture. Stir until combined.

Bake, uncovered, in 9x13 dish at 350 degrees for 30 minutes.

This is the go-to recipe for macaroni and cheese that I make fairly often. I have the recipe memorized and I just eyeball the measurements when I make it. I have written them down here for your convenience. It makes a bunch, since I double the noodles, so this is one of the few recipes that we have leftovers of.

MACARONI AND CHEESE

2 - 16 oz packages of pasta
5 T butter
3 T flour
3 cups milk
8 oz cheddar cheese, shredded
1/4 tsp dry mustard
1 tsp crushed red pepper flakes
Salt and pepper to taste
Chives (optional)

Boil and drain the pasta. Return to pan.

Add butter, flour, and milk. Stir to coat pasta.

Add cheese, dry mustard, red pepper flakes, salt and pepper. Stir and heat until cheese is melted.

Top with chives, if desired.

Couscous Spinach Casserole

Loaded Potato Buffalo Chicken Bake

Lentil Casserole

kind of like casseroles

Tamale Pie

Beef and Bean Dip

Loaded Potato Buffalo Chicken Bake

Easy Creamy Buffalo Chicken Bake

Lentil Casserole

Couscous Spinach Casserole

Black Bean Enchilada Bake

Beans and Rice

Beef and Rice

This is another recipe that doesn't have much of an origin story (I just found it on Pinterest or something), but we love it all the same. The polenta crust makes for a wonderful base ("That's my favorite part," says Ezra), and combined with the other flavors, it makes for an amazing meal.

TAMALE PIE

Cornmeal Base:
1 cup polenta
1-1/2 cups water
1/2 cup milk
1/4 cup cheddar cheese
Salt to taste

Beef Topping:
1 lb ground beef
1/2 tsp oregano
1 tsp cumin
Salt to taste
12 oz salsa
15 oz red kidney beans*
2 T chopped cilantro
8 oz cheddar cheese, shredded

* Could use black beans instead of red kidney beans, especially if that's all you have in the cupboard

Brown the beef in skillet and season with oregano, cumin, and salt. Stir in the salsa, beans, and cilantro. Continue cooking for about 5 minutes so the flavors come together.

While the beef is cooking, put the polenta, water, and milk in a pot and cook on medium heat for about 10 minutes, stirring frequently. When it starts to thicken, stir in the cheese and season with salt. Turn off the heat and let stand for a few minutes to firm up.

Spread the polenta in an even layer at the bottom of a 2 quart casserole dish. Add the beef and bean mixture and top with cheese. Bake, uncovered, at 400 degrees for 20 minutes.

We make this recipe two different ways... sometimes with just beans (say, if I'm feeling cheap or if we need a meal to eat on a Friday during Lent) and sometimes with beef and beans. It's good either way, but adding the meat is probably better.

BEEF AND BEAN DIP

1 lb ground beef
16 oz can refried beans
12 oz salsa
1 cup sour cream
2 cups cheddar cheese, shredded
Tortilla chips

* If making without meat, substitute
   an additional can of refried beans.

Spread refried beans on the bottom of a 2 quart casserole dish. Layer with beef. Mix sour cream with salsa and spread over beef. Top with cheese.

Bake, uncovered, at 350 degrees for 20 minutes.

This is a really yummy and spicy meal. All of the potatoes make it extremely hearty and filling. Remember, if you don't want to use shredded chicken in any of these recipes, just substitute two cubed chicken breasts instead.

LOADED POTATO AND BUFFALO CHICKEN BAKE

1/3 cup olive oil
1-1/2 tsp salt
1 T pepper
1 T paprika
2 T garlic powder
6 T sriracha sauce
10 whole potatoes, cubed
Shredded chicken (see page 18)
8 oz cheddar cheese, shredded
1 cup green onions, diced
8 oz bacon, cooked and crumbled

In a very large bowl, mix together the olive oil, salt, pepper, paprika, garlic powder, and sriracha. Add the cubed potatoes and stir to coat.

Bake the potatoes in a 9x13 baking dish at 450 degrees for 45 minutes, stirring every 15 minutes, until cooked through.

Then, top with shredded chicken, bacon, cheese, and green onion. Return the casserole to the oven and bake for another 15 minutes.

Spicy and delicious are two words that describe this meal. The original recipe called for quinoa, but I've been making it with couscous lately since the price of quinoa seems kind of high. Either way is acceptable and tastes pretty much the same to me.

EASY CREAMY BUFFALO CHICKEN BAKE

3 cups water
1-1/2 cups uncooked couscous
 (or quinoa)
2 small heads broccoli, chopped
Shredded chicken (see page 18)
1 T flour
1 T butter
1-1/2 cups milk
8 oz cheddar cheese
1/4 cup butter
1/2 cup sriracha sauce
1/2 tsp salt
1/4 tsp pepper
4 oz blue cheese, crumbled
Cilantro, for garnish, optional
Chives, for garnish, optional

In a large saucepan, bring couscous and water to a boil. Add broccoli right on top of water, do not stir. Cover and simmer for 10-15 minutes or until water is absorbed. Add chicken.

In medium saucepan, melt 1 T butter over medium heat. Add flour. Whisk together and slowly add milk, stirring as it thickens slightly. Add 1 cup shredded cheddar cheese. Remove from heat and stir in 1/4 cup butter, sriracha sauce, salt, and pepper.

Pour the sauce over couscous mixture and mix together. Transfer to 9x13 baking dish and top with remaining cheddar cheese, sliced.

Bake, uncovered, at 350 degrees for 20 minutes.

Remove from oven and top with blue cheese, and optional fresh cilantro and chives.

This recipe came to us by way of Aileen, who is an excellent cook, lentil maker, and all around human being. She brought this meal to us after Peace was born. It makes a lot, which is great for our hungry family. Which brings me to this important life lesson: whenever somebody you know has a baby, bring them a meal. Always. This is a rule of life.

LENTIL CASSEROLE

1 onion, diced
1 lb dry green lentils
9 cups water
5 carrots, sliced
1 head cauliflower, cut into pieces
1-1/2 cups spinach
1-1/2 tsp cumin
1 tsp coriander
1/4 tsp cayenne
1 tsp basil
2 T balsamic vinegar
1/4 cup butter
Salt to taste

2 cups rice
2 T butter
1/4 tsp red pepper flakes
4 cups watter

In a large saucepan, cook onions. Add lentils and water. Add remaining ingredients (except for the cauliflower and spinach). Bring to a boil and then reduce heat and cover and simmer for 30 minutes. Add cauliflower and spinach, then simmer for 15-20 more minutes until everything is cooked.

Cook rice.

Once the lentils and rice are cooked, put 1/2 of the rice into one 2 quart casserole dish, and 1/2 in another 2 quart casserole dish. Then, put the lentils on top of the rice in each dish.

Bake, uncovered, at 350 degrees for 60 minutes.

Laura M. made this for Book Club, and I just had to have the recipe. It's super good. You can make it with cheese or without. Laura made it with Muenster cheese, but I usually use cheddar, just because that's what I do. Either way is good.

COUSCOUS SPINACH BAKE

2 cups couscous
3 cups boiling water
2 tsp salt
3 cloves garlic, chopped
1 onion, diced
3 tomatoes, diced
2 tsp basil
1/3 cup pine nuts
5 cups spinach
8 oz cheddar cheese, shredded

In a large saucepan, combine couscous, boiling water, and salt. Cover for 5 minutes.

Meanwhile, in a skillet, saute garlic and onion for 5 minutes. Add tomatoes, and cook for 10 minutes more.

Add tomato mixture to couscous. Mix in the rest of the ingredients.

Put in a 9x13 baking dish, top with cheese, and bake, uncovered, at 375 degrees for 25 minutes.

This is another recipe where I use couscous and quinoa pretty much interchangeably (the original called for quinoa). I've noticed how much I use optional chives for topping in a lot of the recipes featured here. That's because we have a chive plant that grows just outside our house and it is easy to get and free of charge. I highly recommend doing this. They grow back every year.

BLACK BEAN ENCHILADA BAKE

1 cup uncooked couscous
2 cups water
1 T butter
1 onion, diced
3 cloves garlic, chopped
1 jalapeno, diced
2 red peppers, diced
1 cup frozen corn
Juice of 1 lime
1 tsp cumin
1 T chili powder
1/3 cup cilantro, chopped
Salt and pepper, to taste
2 - 15 oz cans black beans
12 oz enchilada sauce
2 cups cheddar cheese, shredded
Chives, optional

Add couscous and water to a medium saucepan and bring to a boil over medium heat. Boil for 5 minutes. Turn heat to low and simmer for 15 minutes, or until water is absorbed.

In a large skillet, heat butter over medium heat. Add onion, garlic, and jalapeno. Saute until softened, about 5 minutes. Add in the red peppers and the corn. Cook 3-4 minutes. Add the lime juice, cumin, chili powder, and cilantro. Stir to combine. Season with salt and pepper.

In a 9x13 baking dish, add the cooked couscous and black beans. Add the sauteed vegetable mixture and stir to combine. Pour in the enchilada sauce and 1/2 cup cheddar cheese and stir. Top with remaining cheese.

Bake, covered, at 350 degrees for 20 minutes. Remove foil and bake an additional 10 minutes.

Garnish with chives, if desired.

I've been making this recipe since Ocean was a toddler, and it is one of her favorites, I think, because it's been with her all her life.

BEANS AND RICE

2 cups rice
32 oz tomato juice
1 tsp salt
1/2 tsp pepper
2 tsp cumin
1 tsp chili powder
1 tsp garlic powder
2 - 15 oz cans black beans
Cheddar cheese, optional

Boil rice in tomato juice. When rice is almost completely cooked, add spices and black beans and cook until all of the juice is absorbed.

Top with cheese, if desired.

This is a modification of a favorite recipe my mom used to make when I was growing up, except she made it with pork chops in an electric skillet.

BEEF AND RICE

1 lb ground beef
1 onion, diced
64 oz tomato juice
3 cups rice
1 tsp salt
1 tsp pepper

In a large saucepan, boil rice, tomato juice, salt, and pepper. Cover and simmer for 15 minutes, until rice is cooked.

Meanwhile, brown the ground beef and onion in skillet. Add to rice.

Ground Beef and Potato Curry

Mariah's Curry

Homemade Hamburger Helper

over rice

Mariah's Curry

Beef and Potato Curry

Ground Beef and Lentil Curry

Red Thai Curry Turkey

Sweet Potato Chickpea Curry

Homemade Hamburger Helper

Mongolian Beef

Unstuffed Cabbage Rolls

Chicken a la Bacon

Mariah made this meal for us after Peace was born. The meal had some long name that I can't remember, because we have taken to calling it Mariah's Curry ever since we started making it. I love that we've named this after her, and we can think of her whenever we make it. It's a remarkable curry and one of our favorite meals.

MARIAH'S CURRY

3 T coconut oil
1 onion, diced
1 lb steak, cut up
3 bay leaves
2 tsp cinnamon
6 cardamom pods
8 whole cloves
15 black peppercorns
4 potatoes, cubed
2 carrots, sliced
1/4 tsp tumeric
1 T ground coriander
1/4 tsp cayenne
1 tsp salt
14 oz can coconut milk

Serve over rice

In a large saucepan, heat coconut oil. Cook onion and steak. Add bay leaves, cinnamon, cardamom pods, cloves, and peppercorns.

Add potatoes, carrots, tumeric, coriander, cayenned, salt, and coconut milk. Stir to combine.

Bring to a boil, then cover and simmer for 50 minutes.

Serve over rice. (We use 2 cups rice, 4 cups water.)

Watch out for the cardamom pods. Take them out, either beforehand or while you eat, because you don't want to accidentally eat one of those! Bleck!

This is a fairly new recipe that is quickly becoming a family favorite. I like making curries because, with the rice, they tend to fill us up quite nicely. We cook 2 cups rice with 4 cups water, which seems to be a good amount for us.

BEEF AND POTATO CURRY

1 lb ground beef
1 onion, diced
3 potatoes, cubed
1 jalapeno, diced
1 tsp cinnamon
3 cardamom pods
3 cloves
1 T ginger
2 tsp garlic powder
1 T chili powder
1 T curry powder
1/2 tsp tumeric
Salt to taste
1 tsp vinegar
2 cups water
1 cup frozen peas
14 oz can coconut milk

Serve over rice

In a large saucepan, saute onion, ground beef, jalapeno, and spices.

Add potatoes, water, and vinegar. Cover and simmer for 20 minutes until potatoes are tender.

Add peas and coconut milk. Heat through.

Serve over rice.

This recipe is another recent favorite that we find ourselves making over and over again. It's a great combination of lots of flavors. Not a great origin story with this one... just a recipe I found somewhere on the internet.

GROUND BEEF AND LENTIL CURRY

1 pound ground beef
1 onion
1 T curry powder
1 tsp cumin
1/2 tsp cayenne
1 jalapeno, diced
4 carrots, diced
5 cloves garlic, chopped
15 oz can diced tomatoes
1 cup green lentils
14 oz can coconut milk
2 cups chicken broth
Salt to taste

Serve over rice

In a large saucepan, brown beef with onion and spices. Add jalapeno, carrots, and garlic. Cook for 5 more minutes.

Add remaining ingredients.

Bring to a boil, then cover and simmer for 40 minutes.

Serve over rice.

This recipe calls for ground turkey, but I use ground turkey pretty much interchangeably with ground beef in any given recipe. (It's less expensive than ground beef, so that's why I use it sometimes.) It's a great recipe. It doesn't quite fill us up, so we might have to snack after this meal.

RED THAI CURRY TURKEY

1 lb ground turkey
2 cloves garlic, chopped
4 green onions, sliced
1 red bell pepper, diced
2 tsp red curry paste
Juice of 1 lime
2 T brown sugar
2 tsp fish sauce
14 oz can coconut milk
Cilantro, for garnish

Serve over rice

In a large saucepan, cook ground turkey. Add garlic, green onions, red bell pepper, curry paste, lime juice, sugar, and fish sauce. Stir to combine.

Cover and simmer for 40 minutes.

Add coconut milk and simmer another 10 minutes.

Serve over rice. Garnish with cilantro, if desired.

This is a classic Kuznia recipe that we've made so many times we have kind of gotten tired of it. But it's a good one, and we continue to make it, just not as often as we once did. It's also a great meal to make for anyone who happens to be a gluten-free, dairy-free, vegetarian!

SWEET POTATO CHICKPEA CURRY

1 onion, diced
4 cloves garlic, chopped
1 T ginger
1 T curry powder
1 T chili powder
1 large sweet potato, cubed
15 oz chickpeas (garbanzo beans)
14 oz can coconut milk
1 cup water
Salt to taste

Serve over rice

Saute onion and garlic in a skillet. Stir in ginger, curry powder, and chili powder. Add sweet potato, chickpeas, coconut milk, and water. Bring to a boil, then simmer, covered, for 20 minutes.

Serve over rice.

This recipe came from our friend Elise, when she posted it on her Healing Cuisine blog. Her husband, Dave, used to like packaged Hamburger Helper growing up, so she created a homemade healthy version of it. It's amazingly yummy. (I've altered the recipe slightly.)

HOMEMADE HAMBURGER HELPER

1 lb ground beef
1 onion, diced
1 cup water
4 potatoes, quartered and sliced
14 oz can coconut milk
6 oz can tomato paste
2 tsp garlic powder
1/2 tsp thyme
Salt and pepper to taste

Serve over rice

Cook ground beef and onion in skillet. Remove from pan.

Add 1 cup water, and bring to a boil. Add sliced potatoes, cover, reduce heat, and simmer 6-10 minutes until potatoes are tender.

Uncover and stir in coconut milk, tomato paste, garlic powder, thyme, salt, and pepper. Stir in ground beef and simmer 10 minutes.

Serve over rice.

This is a great recipe. I always like how it looks with the green onions on top. They really make this meal pop! I also want you to know that I use scallions, green onions, and chives interchangeably in pretty much any recipe. I have these perennials growing outside my house (something everyone should do because it's so easy), and just grab whichever looks the best.

MONGOLIAN BEEF

1 pound flank steak, sliced
2 T flour
1/2 cup coconut oil
1/2 cup tamari
1/2 cup brown sugar
3 cloves garlic, chopped
2 tsp ginger
2 green onions, chopped

Serve over rice

In a small saucepan, heat tamari, brown sugar, garlic, and ginger. Bring to a low boil until sauce thickens slightly (about 1-2 minutes).

Place meat in a bowl and coat with flour.

Heat oil in a large skillet. Add beef slices until brown and just cooked.

Add sauce to the beef and stir until sauce becomes thick.

Serve over rice and sprinkle with green onions.

My mom made this meal for us after Solomon was born (among a bunch of other meals, bless her heart for taking care of us so well). I liked this because it was a TON easier to make than the regular cabbage rolls I had made in the past. It's easy and delicious!

UNSTUFFED CABBAGE ROLLS

1 lb ground beef
1 onion, diced
4 cloves garlic, chopped
6 oz can tomato paste
2 cups chicken broth
1 small head cabbage, chopped
Salt and pepper to taste

Serve over rice

In a large saucepan, cook ground beef and onion. Add garlic and cook one minute more.

Add the chicken broth, chopped cabbage, tomato sauce, salt, and pepper. Bring to a boil. Cover and simmer 20-30 minutes, or until cabbage is tender.

Serve over rice.

We love this combination of ingredients, ever so flavorful and delicious. It's quick to make, with the slicing of the vegetables keeping you busy the entire time.

CHICKEN A LA BACON

8 oz bacon, chopped
1 onion, diced
2 leeks, sliced
10 oz mushrooms, sliced
1 red bell pepper, diced
Shredded chicken (see page 18)
1/2 cup white wine
14 oz can coconut milk

Serve over rice

Cook chopped bacon and set aside.

In a large skillet, cook onion and leeks until tender, about 5 minutes. Add chicken, mushrooms, and red bell pepper and cook for another 5 minutes.

Add white wine and cook until wine is reduced by half.

Add coconut milk. Season with salt and pepper. Cook through.

Serve over rice.

Popcorn Salad

Beef and Bulgur Salad

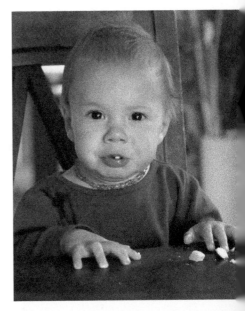

Egg Salad

main salads

Beef and Bulgur Salad

Taco Pasta Salad

Popcorn Salad

Egg Salad

This is a great summertime recipe for us. It's quick and easy to make, and doesn't heat up the whole kitchen when making it. I sometimes use a can of diced tomatoes with green chilies if I deem fresh tomatoes "out of season" or "too expensive". (The reverse of that is that I often use fresh tomatoes in recipes that call for canned, so just do as you see fit.)

BEEF AND BULGUR SALAD

1 cup bulgur
2 cups water
1 lb ground beef
1 onion, diced
4 cloves garlic, chopped
2 tsp cumin
1 tsp salt
3/4 tsp ground pepper
2 tomatoes, diced
1/4 cup fresh cilantro, chopped
1 head iceberg lettuce, chopped

Boil bulgur in 2 cups water. Cover and simmer until cooked, about 10 minutes.

In skillet, cook ground beef, onions, garlic, cumin, salt, and pepper. Add diced tomatoes and cilantro.

Add cooked bulgur to the skillet and stir to combine. Add more salt and pepper, if desired.

Remove from heat and serve immediately over beds of lettuce.

This is a great make ahead meal that we make on days we have volleyball or basketball games and will be getting home late. All we have to do is take it out of the fridge and eat. Feel free to add scallions, green onions, or chives. I use them pretty much interchangeably.

TACO PASTA SALAD

16 oz pasta
2 - 15 oz cans black beans
2 cups frozen corn
1/2 cup fresh cilantro, chopped
2 tomatoes, diced
12 oz salsa
1/3 cup olive oil
Juice of one lime
2 tsp cumin
2 tsp chili powder
2 cloves garlic, chopped
Salt and pepper, to taste
8 oz cheddar cheese, shredded
2 avocados, diced (optional)
Scallions (optional)

Cook pasta. Drain and cool.

In a large bowl, add the cooled pasta, black beans, corn, cilantro, tomatoes, and salsa. Toss gently.

In a small bowl, whisk together olive oil, lime juice, cumin, chili powder, and garlic. Pour over pasta and toss to coat. Salt and pepper to taste. Chill until serving.

Right before serving, toss in the cheese and avocado.

This is the strangest meal that you are going to find in this cookbook, but we actually enjoy it very much. We first had it at a block party when we lived with Uncle Vince. Somebody served it, and we were, like, "What the heck?" I went home and wanted to learn more about this strange concoction (sure enough, it is a thing), and we've been making it ever since.

POPCORN SALAD

8 oz bacon, cooked and chopped
3/4 cup mayo (see recipe below)
1 cup celery, diced
8 oz cheddar cheese, shredded
1/4 cup carrots, diced
2 T chives, chopped
8 oz can water chestnuts
12 cups popped popcorn

Mix everything together.

Seriously, that's all there is to it.

Oh, yeah, and enjoy (I think)!

Homemade Mayo Recipe:

2 egg yolks
1 tsp dry mustard
1 T apple cider vinegar
1/2 tsp salt
1-1/4 cup olive oil

Mix first four ingredients together, and then SLOWLY add olive oil while whisking continuously.

Another great, easy to make, summertime recipe. We have this for lunch sometimes, when we want something a little different from our usual meat and cheese sandwiches. The homemade mayo makes this extra special.

EGG SALAD

6 hard-boiled eggs, diced
2 celery stalks, diced
1/2 onion, diced
1 carrot, diced
1/3 cup mayo (see recipe below)
Salt and pepper, to taste
Chives (optional)

Mix everything together.

Serve on toast.

Homemade Mayo Recipe:

2 egg yolks
1 tsp dry mustard
1 T apple cider vinegar
1/2 tsp salt
1-1/4 cup olive oil

Mix first four ingredients together, and then SLOWLY add olive oil while whisking continuously.

Beef Bourguignon

Cream Cheese F

Beef Bourguignon

Bacon and Cheese Grits

Cream Cheese Enchiladas

Tortilla Pie

Ratatouille

Pizza

After going to a Julia Child storytime at the Red Balloon Bookstore, I decided to check out a cookbook from Julia Child. I came upon her recipe for Beef Bourguignon, which I have since dumbed down and made easier and cheaper (as I always do). It is delicious. I usually make it after I host a gathering and people leave behind their red wine.

BEEF BOURGUIGNON

8 oz bacon, chopped
1 lb stew meat, cut up
3 carrots, sliced
1 onion, diced
1 T tomato paste
4 cloves garlic, chopped
1 tsp thyme
1 bay leaf
2 T flour
2-3 cups red wine
2-3 cups chicken broth
10 oz white mushrooms, quartered
2 T butter

Cook bacon and set aside.

In a Dutch oven, brown stew meat, carrots, and onion. Add tomato paste, garlic, thyme, bay leaf, red wine, chicken broth, and flour. Salt and pepper to taste.

Cover and place in a 300 degree oven and let cook for 2-3 hours.

Cook mushrooms in the 2 T of butter. Add to the pot and simmer on stovetop for 15 minutes.

If there is too much liquid, add 1-2 more tablespoons of flour to thicken.

This recipe came to us by way of Erin P. She is an amazing cook and baker. I made a difficult cake she recommended once, and it wasn't turning out quite right, to which Ezra said, "Well, you're no Erin P." True enough. But at least I dumbed this recipe down to make it easy enough for me to make (the original called for shrimp and pancetta, just fyi).

BACON AND CHEESE GRITS

2 leeks, sliced
1 T butter
2 cloves garlic, chopped
1 green bell pepper, diced
3 cups chicken broth
1 tsp salt
1 cup quick-cooking grits
8 oz cheddar cheese, shredded
8 oz bacon
1/4 tsp cayenne

Cook bacon and set aside.

In a large saucepan, cook leeks in butter until softened, about 4-5 minutes. Add garlic and green pepper, and saute another 3-4 minutes.

Add chicken broth and salt. Bring to a boil. Whisk in the grits, return to boil, then reduce heat and simmer, partially covered, until broth has been absorbed, about 5 minutes.

Add 1 cup of the cheese, cayenne, and stir to melt. Salt and pepper, to taste.

Distribute grits mixture among bowls. Top with bacon and remaining cheese and serve.

This recipe always reminds me of how Ezra would make it in the weeks and months after Solomon was born. It became kind of his go-to recipe. It is yummy and delicious, and it tastes even better when Ezra makes it.

CREAM CHEESE ENCHILADAS

8 oz cream cheese
12 oz salsa
8 oz cheddar cheese, shredded
2 - 14 oz cans black beans
1 cup frozen corn
1/2 tsp chili powder
1/4 tsp cumin
Salt and pepper to taste
10 tortillas
Chives

In a medium bowl, mix together cream cheese, half the salsa, and half the cheddar cheese. In a second bowl, toss together the black beans, corn, cumin, chili powder, salt, pepper, and chives.

Add bean mixture to the cheese mixture and stir to combine.

Spread about 1/2 cup salsa in the bottom of a 9x13 baking dish.

Place 1/3 to 1/2 cup filling on a tortilla. Roll up and put in dish seam side down. Repeat process for remaining tortillas.

Pour remaining salsa over enchiladas, spreading to coat all of them. Top with remaining cheddar cheese.

Bake, uncovered, at 350 for 20-25 minutes.

Sprinkle with chives and serve.

This is rather sloppy and a pain to cut into, but it tastes delicious and looks rather nice if you do it properly. Sometimes I'll divide it into two pies with 5 tortillas each. That helps it to stay together a bit better.

TORTILLA PIE

1 - 14 oz can pinto beans
12 oz salsa, divided
1 tsp garlic powder
2 T cilantro
2 - 14 oz cans black beans
2 tomatoes, diced
10 tortillas
8 oz cheddar cheese, shredded

In a large bowl, mash pinto beans. Stir in 3/4 cup salsa and garlic.

In a separate bowl, mix together 1/4 cup salsa, cilantro, black beans, and tomatoes.

Place one tortilla in a pie plate. Spread 3/4 cup pinto bean mixture over tortilla. Top with 1/4 cup cheese, and cover with another tortilla. Spread with 3/4 cup black bean mixture. Repeat layering.

Cover with foil and bake at 400 degrees for 40 minutes.

This is another recipe brought to us by way of Sarah R. She brought us this meal after Peace was born. I've been making it every year at harvest time ever since. It's a great way to use all of the vegetables that are in season that time of year. Since Sarah served it to us over spaghetti, I do the same.

RATATOUILLE

1 onion, diced
4 cloves garlic, chopped
1 T butter
1 medium eggplant, cubed
2 green peppers, diced
3 zucchini, sliced
4 tomatoes, diced
1 tsp salt
1/4 tsp pepper
1 tsp oregano
1/2 tsp thyme

16 oz spaghetti, cooked

In a large saucepan, saute onion and garlic in butter for 2 minutes. Add eggplant and saute for 5 minutes. Add green peppers and cook for another 5 minutes. Add zucchini and cook for 5 more minutes, then add seasonings and tomatoes. Cover and simmer for 30 minutes.

Serve over spaghetti.

This is a very basic pizza recipe. It is a lunch staple for us. We have it once a week. We make it simply and easily by using half a jar of Trader Joe's spaghetti sauce (and then I use the remaining half jar for pizza the next week). You could also use canned pizza sauce, but it is less expensive this way.

Pizza Dough:
2-1/2 tsp dry yeast
1 T sugar
1 cup warm water
3 cups flour
1 tsp salt
2 T olive oil

13 oz spaghetti sauce
8 oz cheddar cheese, shredded

For dough, dissolve yeast and sugar in warm water. Let sit for 5 minutes. Then, add the flour, salt, and olive oil. Knead the dough for 5 minutes, and then spread on a greased cookie sheet (one that has edges, ours is 12x17).

Spread 13 oz of spaghetti sauce (half a jar) over the dough. Top with cheese.

Bake at 425 degrees for 13 minutes.

Potato Salad

Birds Nests

Butternut Squash Casserole

Butternut Squash Casserole

Potato Salad

Apple Quinoa Salad

Smoothie

Kombucha

Birds Nests

Pumpkin Bread Pudding

Rhubarb Ice Cream

This recipe came to us from my dear friend, Kelly C. She made it for a blessingway once, and the recipe has been passed around our parenting community so many times that this dish has become a bit of a mainstay at important gatherings. It just doesn't feel like an event unless someone brings this dish.

BUTTERNUT SQUASH CASSEROLE

1 butternut squash, cubed
1 red bell pepper, cut up
3 T olive oil
2 cloves garlic, chopped
3 T fresh parsley, chopped
2 tsp fresh rosemary, chopped
Salt and pepper, to taste
2 oz Parmesan, grated
4 oz feta cheese

In a VERY large bowl, mix together squash, bell pepper, oil, garlic, and herbs. Transfer to 9x13 pan and sprinkle with Parmesan.

Bake, uncovered, at 400 degrees for 40-45 minutes or until squash is tender.

Top with crumbled feta cheese before serving.

Nothing reminds me of summer more than this homemade potato salad. We bring it often to potlucks in the summer. Vernon usually ends up making it, which I especially like (because I always enjoy food more when someone else makes it). I think one of the things that makes it so fresh and tasty is the fact that we make our mayo from scratch. Yum!

POTATO SALAD

2 lbs potatoes, cubed
2 T plus 2 tsp apple cider vinegar
6 T olive oil
4 hard-boiled eggs
6 cloves garlic, chopped
1/2 onion, diced
3 celery stalks, chopped
1/4 cup mayo (see recipe below)
1 tsp salt
1 tsp pepper

Cook potatoes. Cool and let dry.

Whisk oil, garlic, onion, and apple cider vinegar in a small bowl. Add 2 hard-boiled egg yolks and mash. Coarsely chop remaining eggs and egg whites.

Add everything to the potatoes and mix well.

Homemade Mayo Recipe:

2 egg yolks
1 tsp dry mustard
1 T apple cider vinegar
1/2 tsp salt
1-1/4 cup olive oil

Mix first four ingredients together, and then SLOWLY add olive oil while whisking continuously.

This is a deliciously refreshing salad that I sometimes make if I ever need a side dish or something kind of fancy to bring to a party. This is another recipe from Elise (although I altered it a bit), who makes recipes up herself because she's talented like that.

APPLE QUINOA SALAD

2 cups quinoa
4 cups water
2 T onion, diced
2 tsp curry powder
1/2 tsp salt
4 T olive oil
1 granny smith apple
1/4 cup fresh mint leaves, chopped
1/4 cup slivered almonds

Boil quinoa and water. Cover and simmer for 15 minutes. Let cool.

Whisk together onion, curry powder, and salt. SLOWLY whisk in olive oil until dressing is emulsified.

Add quinoa, 1/2 of the granny smith apple diced, mint, and almonds. Mix well to combine.

Thinly slice remaining 1/2 of apple for presentation.

Vernon makes us a smoothie almost every morning. He has tried a handful of smoothie recipes over the years, but seems to have settled on this one.

SMOOTHIE

1/2 cup kefir
1/2 cup water
3 eggs
1 banana
1/4 avocado
3 T sugar
2 T flaxseed
2 T cocoa powder
2 carrots
10 ice cubes
Handful of kale (optional)

Put everything in a blender and blend. Add extra water when blending if needed.

(Vern adds in the banana peel if it is organic.)

Kombucha is starting to become trendy now, but we have been making it for years. If you ever need a scoby, come to me, I'll probably always have one ready for you. If I don't, I'll know where to find one.

KOMBUCHA

3 quarts water
1 cup sugar
4 black tea bags

Scoby

Bring 3 quarts water to boil. Add sugar. Stir to dissolve. Add tea bags. Steep until cooled. (I usually leave it overnight.)

Pour mixture into a 4 quart bowl or jar. Add scoby and 1/2 cup of previously brewed kombucha. Let sit, covered with a towel that is secured by a rubber band, in a dark place for 1-2 weeks. (The warmer it is outside, the less time it will take to ferment. So, as a general guideline, I ferment for around 1 week in the summer, and 2 weeks or more in the winter.)

Pour into bottles.

If you'd like to make flavored kombucha (which I do), add 1/4 cup of juice to each bottle and let sit for another 5-7 days.

Transfer to refrigerator and serve cold.

Lindsay M. made this for Mom's Night Out once and I've been enamored with it ever since. Once you're old enough, you can add a splash of dark rum to it. That will really make the flavors pop.

PUMPKIN WHITE HOT CHOCOLATE

4 cups milk
1 cup white chocolate chips
2 T cornstarch
6 T pumpkin puree
2 T vanilla

Mix and melt in a saucepan over low heat.

Ladle into mugs and serve.

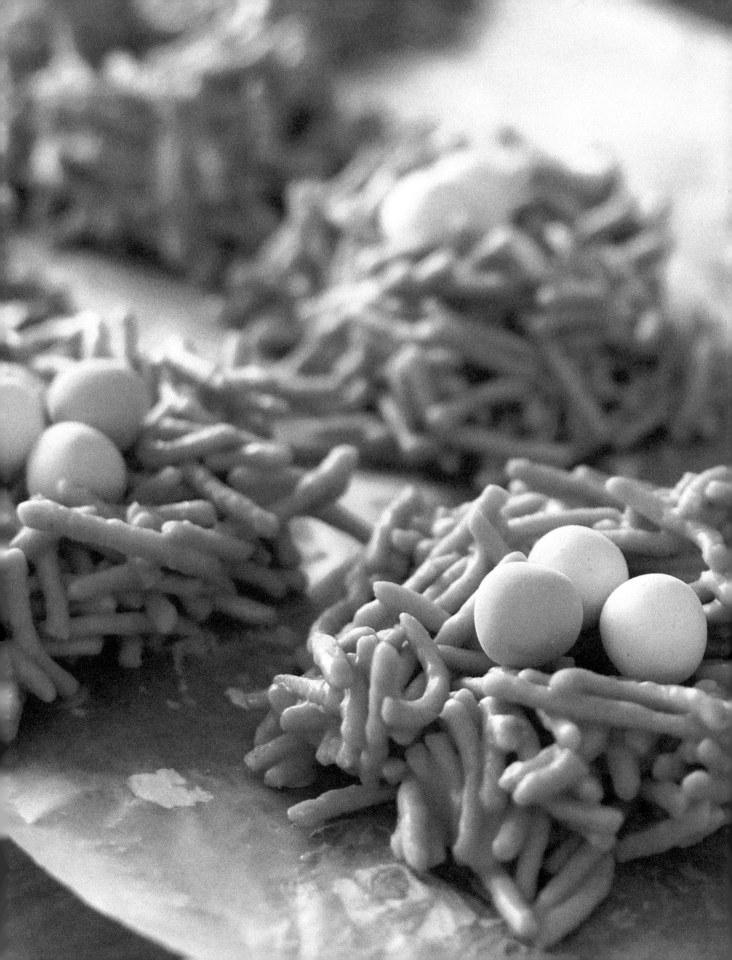

It is our tradition to make these every spring after spotting the first robin of the year. I love this tradition! It's a way to mark the changing of the seasons with food and fun. My mom used to make these for Easter when I was a kid, so they always make me think of her. I've changed the recipe a bit in an attempt to make them more healthy.

BIRDS NESTS

12 oz chow mein noodles
1 cup peanut butter
1/2 cup coconut oil
1/2 cup honey
Egg-shaped candy

Melt peanut butter, coconut oil, and honey in a large saucepan. Stir in chow mein noodles.

Form into nests on a wax paper lined cookie sheet. Put into freezer to harden.

Put egg-shaped type candy into nests before serving.

Other than birthdays, we hardly ever make desserts. But this is one that we make once a year during the month of October, simply because it is so good and reminds us of October. (Again, us and our pumpkin recipes! What can I say? We love pumpkin.)

PUMPKIN BREAD PUDDING

2 cups half and half
2 cups pureed pumpkin
1 cup brown sugar
2 eggs
2 tsp cinnamon
1/2 tsp ground cloves
1/2 tsp allspice
1/4 tsp nutmeg
1/4 tsp ginger
2 tsp vanilla extract
10 cups - 1/2 inch cubed egg bread

Caramel Sauce
1 cup brown sugar
1/2 cup butter
1/2 cup cream

Whisk half and half, pumpkin, brown sugar, spices, and vanilla extract in a large bowl. Fold in bread cubes.

Transfer mixture to 9x13 baking dish. Let s tand for 15 minutes, then bake, uncovered, at 350 degrees for 40 minutes.

For caramel sauce, whisk brown sugar and butter in saucepan over medium heat until butter melts. Whisk in cream and stir until sugar dissolves and sauce is smooth, about 3 minutes.

Serve warm with caramel sauce

We have been making homemade ice cream on Sundays during the summer for the past three years. We call it Ice Cream Sunday. This recipe is one of our favorites. We use fresh rhubarb that grows in our yard. We got the rhubarb from our next-door neighbor, 86-year-old Charles Schwaab, who passed away earlier this year.

RHUBARB ICE CREAM

3 cups sliced fresh rhubarb
1 cup sugar
Juice from 1 lemon
2 cups cream

In a 9x13 baking dish, combine rhubarb and sugar. Bake, covered, at 375 degrees for 20 minutes, or until tender, stirring occasionally. Cool slightly.

Place rhubarb mixture in a blender and blend. Transfer to a bowl. Refrigerate, covered, until cold.

Stir lemon juice into rhubarb.

In a small bowl, beat cream until stiff peaks form. Fold into rhubarb mixture. Freeze 1 hour, stirring every 15 minutes. Freeze, covered, overnight.

Lotion

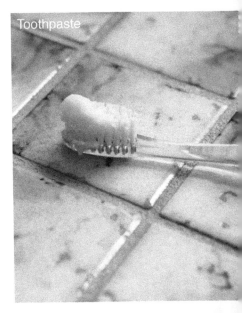

Toothpaste

Detergent

miscellaneous

Detergent

Toothpaste

Deodorant

Sugar Scrub

Lotion

DETERGENT

1-1/2 cup baking soda
1-1/2 cup washing soda
1/2 cup Epsom salt
2 T salt

Mix together. Use 1 T per load.

TOOTHPASTE

4 T coconut oil
6 T baking soda
1 drop peppermint essential oil

Mix together. (Use a fork if the
coconut oil is hard.)

DEODORANT

3 T coconut oil
3 T shea butter
1/2 tsp baking soda
3 drops lavender essential oil

Mix together.

SUGAR SCRUB

1/2 cup coconut oil, melted
1-1/2 cup sugar
1/4 cup kosher salt
5 drops lavender essential oil

Mix together.

LOTION

1-1/4 cup coconut oil
1/2 cup beeswax
10 drops lavender essential oil

Melt coconut oil and beeswax in a jar in gently simmering water. Do not let it boil. Stir occasionally.

Remove from heat.

Keep stirring as the mixture cools and solidifies. This is the key to making the lotion creamy.

Once the mixture is cool but still stirrable, add in the essential oil.

RECIPE INDEX

Lightning Source UK Ltd.
Milton Keynes UK
UKHW051604111019
351368UK00002B/22/P